COOL COOKING UP CHILI

Beyond the Basics for Kids Who Cook

LISA
WAGNER

A Division of ABDO

ABDO
Publishing Company

Visit us at www.abdopublishing.com

Published by ABDO Publishing Company, P.O. Box 398166, Minneapolis, MN 55439. Copyright ©2014 by Abdo Consulting Group, Inc. International copyrights reserved in all countries. No part of this book may be reproduced in any form without written permission from the publisher. The Checkerboard Library™ is a trademark and logo of ABDO Publishing Company.

Printed in the United States of America,
North Mankato, Minnesota
102013
012014

 PRINTED ON RECYCLED PAPER

Editor: Liz Salzmann
Content Developer: Nancy Tuminelly
Cover and Interior Design and Production:
Colleen Dolphin, Mighty Media, Inc.
Food Production: Desirée Bussiere
Photo Credits: Colleen Dolphin, Shutterstock

Library of Congress Cataloging-in-Publication Data
Wagner, Lisa, 1958- author.
  Cool cooking up chili : beyond the basics for kids who cook / Lisa Wagner.
     pages cm. -- (Cool young chefs)
  Audience: Ages 8 to 12.
  Includes index.
  ISBN 978-1-62403-087-1
1. Chili con carne--Juvenile literature. 2. Cooking, American--Juvenile literature. I. Title.
  TX749.W243 2014
  641.82'36--dc23
                          2013022527

TO ADULT HELPERS

Congratulations on being the proud parent of an up-and-coming chef! This series of books is designed for children who have already done some cooking—most likely with your guidance and encouragement. Now, with some of the basics out of the way, it's time to really get cooking!

The focus of this series is on parties and special events. The "Big Idea" is all about the creative side of cooking (mastering a basic method or recipe and then using substitutions to create original recipes). Listening to your young chef's ideas for new creations and sharing your own ideas and experiences can lead to exciting (and delicious) discoveries!

While the recipes are designed to let children cook independently as much as possible, you'll need to set some ground rules for using the kitchen, tools, and ingredients. Most importantly, adult supervision is a must whenever a child uses the stove, oven, or sharp tools. Look for these symbols:

Your assistance, patience, and praise will pay off with tasty rewards for the family, and invaluable life skills for your child. Let the adventures in cooking beyond the basics begin!

CONTENTS

HOST A CHILI PARTY!

Welcome to Cool Young Chefs! If you have already used other Cool Cooking books, this series is for you. You know how to read a recipe and how to prepare ingredients. You have learned about measuring, cooking tools, and kitchen safety. Best of all, you like to cook!

This book is all about chili and tasty things to serve with it. Chili is a popular main dish. Kids and adults love it! It is a perfect dish to serve at a party too. Cook a big pot of chili, make coleslaw, and bake some corn bread muffins. Set out several toppings and let your guests get creative. Just like that, you have a Fix-Your-Own-Chili Party!

FEED A CROWD

If you have a big crowd, it is easy to make a bigger batch of chili. The chili recipes in this book can be made using two times the amount of each ingredient. This is called "doubling the recipe."

DO-AHEAD RECIPES

You can make your chili the day before you plan to serve it. When you reheat the chili, the flavors will be even better!

CHILI COOK-OFF

A chili cook-off is an event where people taste many kinds of chili. You can host one in your own home! Invite your friends to bring their favorite chili. You provide bowls, silverware, and toppings. Put a sheet of paper and a pencil next to each pot of chili. Ask people to give each chili one to four stars. The chili that gets the most stars wins! You can ask your guests to bring copies of their recipes. Share these with all of the guests. That way everyone wins!

WHAT'S THE BIG IDEA?

Besides being a good cook, a chef is prepared, **efficient**, organized, resourceful, creative, and adventurous. The Big Idea in *Cool Cooking Up Chili* is all about being efficient.

Being efficient means keeping things simple. The chili recipes in this book require very few tools. Only one pot is needed to cook a big batch of chili. Cleanup is easy when you only use a few tools and one pot!

Saving time and effort is efficient. Instead of measuring spices each time you make chili, do it once! The recipe for Homemade Chili Seasoning makes enough seasoning for a few batches of chili. Keep it in a covered container and you will be ready to make chili any time! You can also use it to season meat or beans for **tacos**.

Being efficient also means not wasting anything. If you make too much chili you will never have to waste it. Chili can be frozen for weeks and it will still taste great. Freeze chili in a plastic freezer bag. Or use a plastic container with a tight lid. Anything you put in the freezer should already be cold. The best way to do this is to put it in the refrigerator overnight first.

FIRST THINGS FIRST

A successful chef is smart, careful, and patient. Take time to review the basics before you start cooking. After that, get creative and have some fun!

BE SMART, BE SAFE

- Start with clean hands, tools, and work surfaces.
- Always get **permission** to use the kitchen, cooking tools, and ingredients.
- Ask an adult when you need help or have questions.
- Always have an adult nearby when you use the stove, oven, or sharp tools.
- Prevent accidents by working slowly and carefully.

NO GERMS ALLOWED

After you handle raw eggs or raw meat, wash your hands with soap and water. Wash tools and work surfaces with soap and water too. Raw eggs and raw meat have bacteria that don't survive when the food is cooked. But the bacteria can survive at room or body temperature. These bacteria can make you very sick if you consume them. So, keep everything clean!

BE PREPARED

- Read through the entire recipe before you do anything else!
- Gather all the tools and ingredients you will need.
- Wash fruits and vegetables well. Pat them dry with a **towel**.
- Get the ingredients ready. The list of ingredients tells how to prepare each item.
- If you see a word you don't know, check the **glossary** on page 30.
- Do the steps in the order they are listed.

GOOD COOKING TAKES TIME

- Allow plenty of time to prepare your recipes.
- Be patient with yourself. **Prep** work can take a long time at first.

ONE LAST THING

- When you are done cooking, wash all the dishes and **utensils**.
- Clean up your work area and put away any unused ingredients.

KEY SYMBOLS

In this book, you will see some symbols beside the recipes. Here is what they mean.

The recipe requires the use of a stove or oven. You need adult **supervision** and assistance.

A sharp tool such as a peeler, knife, or **grater** is needed. Be extra careful, and get an adult to stand by.

BEYOND COOL

Remember the Big Idea? In the Beyond Cool boxes, you will find ideas to help you create your own recipes. Once you learn a recipe, you will be able to make many **versions** of it. Remember, being able to make original recipes turns cooks into chefs!

When you modify a recipe, be sure to write down what you did. If anyone asks for your recipe, you will be able to share it proudly.

GET THE PICTURE

When a step number in a recipe has a circle around it with an arrow, it points to the picture that shows how to do the step.

③ ⟶

COOL TIP

These tips can help you do something faster, better, or more easily.

UNIQUELY COOL

Here are some of the **techniques**, ingredients, and toppings used in this book.

TECHNIQUES:

CUT THE KERNELS OFF CORNCOBS

Hold a corncob upright on a cutting board. Cut down the side of the cob with a sharp knife. Turn the cob and cut again. Repeat until you've gone all the way around the cob.

CORE AND SLICE CABBAGE

Hold the cabbage on a cutting board with the core facing up. Slice down through the core to cut the cabbage in half. Cut each half in half again. Set each piece on its side and cut off the core. Throw the pieces of core away. Cut the rest of the cabbage into thin strips.

MAKE ZEST

Zest is small pieces of citrus peel. Make it by rubbing the side of the citrus fruit with a zester. Or use the smallest holes on a **grater**.

INGREDIENTS:

DRY MUSTARD

BLACK, PINTO, AND KIDNEY BEANS

YELLOW CORNMEAL

WHITE CORNMEAL

TOPPING IDEAS:

TORTILLA
CHIPS

PICKLED
JALAPEÑOS

SOUR
CREAM

LIME
WEDGES

BLACK
OLIVES

SCALLIONS

GUACAMOLE

CILANTRO

HOT SAUCE

WHITE ONION

SALSA

GRATED
CHEESE

HOMEMADE CHILI SEASONING

MAKES 1½ CUPS

ingredients

12 tablespoons ancho chile powder

2 teaspoons garlic powder

2 teaspoons onion powder

1 teaspoon cayenne pepper

4 teaspoons dried oregano

2 tablespoons paprika

4 tablespoons ground cumin

2 tablespoons salt or garlic salt

2 teaspoons black pepper

tools

measuring spoons

small mixing bowl

fork

jar with lid or other covered container

 1 Put all of the ingredients in a bowl. Mix well.

2 Store in a closed jar or covered container at room temperature.

Chile Powder & Chili Seasoning

There is a difference between chile (spelled with an "e") and chili (spelled with an "i"). A chile is a pepper. Chile powder is dried chiles that have been ground into a powder. Chili is a stew made with chiles and meat or beans.

Because there are many kinds of chile peppers, there are many **varieties** of chile powder. Some are mild and some are very hot! The recipes in this book use ancho chile powder. Ancho chiles are dried poblano peppers. Ancho chile powder adds mild to medium heat to a dish.

You can use other kinds of chile powder instead. Paprika is a very mild chile powder. Cayenne is also a type of chile powder, but it is very hot. If you use cayenne instead of ancho chile powder, use just a tiny bit. Cayenne is more than 10 times hotter than ancho chile powder!

Use mild chile powder in your recipes at first. See how you and your family like it. If want your food to be a little hotter, try using medium chile powder.

Chili seasoning, sometimes called chili powder, is a mixture of chile powder and other spices. It is used for making chili. Make your own Homemade Chili Seasoning to use in other recipes.

BEYOND COOL

You can vary the amounts of the different spices. Make sure chile powder is your main ingredient, then have some fun! Increase or **decrease** the amounts of any of the other spices. For a hotter chili seasoning, add more cayenne and some red pepper flakes. For a milder seasoning, **omit** the cayenne and add more paprika.

THE BEST BLACK BEAN CHILI

ingredients

1 tablespoon vegetable oil

1 medium onion, diced

1 red or green bell pepper, diced

3 cloves garlic, minced

1 cup fresh or frozen corn kernels

1 4-ounce can chopped green chiles

3 15-ounce cans black beans, drained and rinsed

1 28-ounce can diced tomatoes

3 tablespoons Homemade Chili Seasoning (page 12)

tools

measuring spoons

measuring cups

sharp knife

cutting board

can opener

strainer

large pot with lid

mixing spoon

1 Heat the oil in a large pot over medium heat. Sauté the onion for 5 minutes. Add the bell pepper and sauté for 5 more minutes. Add the garlic and sauté for 1 more minute.

2 Stir in the corn and green chiles.

3 Stir in the beans, diced tomatoes, chili seasoning and 1 cup water.

4 Turn the heat to low. Cover the pot. Let it simmer for 45 minutes.

COOL TIP

Want your chili to be spicier? Just add more chili seasoning.

BEYOND COOL

- For a colorful chili, use a mix of red and green bell pepper.

- Add other vegetables, such as zucchini, celery, or carrots.

- Use more than one kind of beans. A combination of black beans, kidney beans, and pinto beans makes a **delicious** chili!

- One **minced** jalapeño pepper will really spice up your chili. Be careful! Wear rubber gloves when you cut jalapeños, because these peppers are hot! When you are done chopping, be sure to wash your work surface and knife well.

HARDY CHILI CON CARNE

a.k.a. Chili with Meat

ingredients

2 tablespoons vegetable oil

1 large onion, chopped

3 stalks celery, sliced

3 cloves garlic, minced

1 red or green bell pepper, diced

1 pound lean ground beef or turkey

1 28-ounce can diced tomatoes with liquid

4 tablespoons Homemade Chili Seasoning (page 12)

2 15-ounce cans red kidney beans, rinsed and drained

tools

measuring spoons

measuring cups

sharp knife

cutting board

can opener

strainer

large pot with lid

mixing spoon

16

1 Heat the oil in a large pot over medium heat. Sauté the onion, celery, and garlic for 5 minutes. Add the bell pepper and sauté for 5 more minutes.

2 Add the meat and break it up into small pieces. Cook and stir until the meat is fully cooked. Meat is fully cooked when all the pink color is gone.

3 Stir in the diced tomatoes, chili seasoning, and 1 cup water. Cover and simmer over very low heat for 40 minutes. Stir the chili every 10 minutes.

4 Stir in the kidney beans and cook for 15 more minutes.

BEYOND COOL

- For spicier chili with a smoky flavor, add one or two finely chopped chipotle peppers. Canned chipotle peppers are smoked jalapeños packed in adobo sauce. You can use the adobo sauce as a seasoning too.

- You can also increase the heat by adding more chili seasoning.

COOL TIP

Make it a meal! Serve the chili over cooked white rice. Cook the rice according to the instructions on the package. **Garnish** with your favorite toppings.

CHOW DOWN CHICKEN CHILI

ingredients

3 cans Great Northern or Cannellini beans, drained and rinsed

2 tablespoons olive oil

1 large onion, chopped

4 cloves garlic, minced

1 pound cooked chicken breast, shredded

1 quart chicken broth

2 4-ounce cans chopped green chile peppers

2 teaspoons ground cumin

1 teaspoon dried oregano

½ teaspoon cayenne pepper

salt

black pepper

1½ cups grated Monterey Jack cheese

tools

measuring spoons

measuring cups

sharp knife

cutting board

can opener

strainer

medium bowl

fork

large pot with lid

mixing spoon

1. Put one-third of the beans in a medium bowl. Use a fork to mash the beans into a paste.

2. Heat the oil in a large pot over medium heat. Sauté the onion and garlic for 10 minutes.

3. Add the chicken, broth, green chiles, cumin, oregano, and cayenne. Stir well and bring to a boil.

4. Reduce heat to low. Add the mashed beans plus the whole beans to the pot. Simmer for 30 minutes.

5. Add salt and black pepper to taste. Cover and simmer for 45 minutes.

6. Top each serving with **grated** Monterey Jack cheese.

COOL TIP

You can use ground chicken instead of chicken breast. After step 2, add the ground chicken but not the broth. Break up the chicken into small pieces using a rubber spatula. Cook until all the pink is gone. Then add the broth and spices.

BUTTERMILK CORN BREAD MUFFINS

HOT STUFF!

ingredients

vegetable oil

2 cups yellow cornmeal

1½ teaspoons baking powder

½ teaspoon baking soda

1 teaspoon salt

3 tablespoons sugar

1 egg, lightly beaten with a fork

1½ cups buttermilk

2 tablespoons butter

tools

12-cup muffin pan

measuring cups

measuring spoons

fork

large mixing bowl

mixing spoon

small microwave-safe bowl

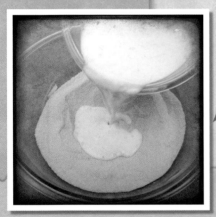

1. Preheat the oven to 450 degrees. Grease the inside of the muffin cups with vegetable oil.

2. Mix the cornmeal, baking powder, baking soda, salt, and sugar together in a large bowl.

3. Put the butter in small microwave-safe bowl. Cook in microwave on high for 30 seconds. If the butter is not all melted, cook for 20 more seconds.

4. Add the beaten egg and buttermilk to the butter and stir well.

5. Make a hole in the cornmeal mixture and pour in the butter mixture. Stir just until the dry and wet ingredients are blended together. Divide the batter evenly in the greased muffin cups.

6. Bake for 15 minutes.

BEYOND COOL

- For spicy corn bread, add some chile powder to the dry ingredients.
- You can use white cornmeal instead of yellow, or a combination of yellow and white.

COOL TIP

You can also use a 9 × 9-inch baking pan or 10-inch ovenproof **skillet** instead of a muffin pan. Increase the baking time to 20 to 25 minutes.

SAUCY COLESLAW TWO WAYS

ingredients

ORANGE VINAIGRETTE COLESLAW

1 green cabbage, thinly sliced

3 carrots, peeled and grated

6 scallions, thinly sliced

3 ears of fresh corn, kernels cut from cob

1 red bell pepper, diced

½ cup chopped cilantro

DRESSING

½ cup fresh squeezed orange juice

zest of one orange

¼ cup rice vinegar (unseasoned)

¼ cup canola or vegetable oil

salt and pepper to taste

CREAMY COLESLAW

1 green cabbage, thinly sliced

3 carrots, peeled, grated

6 scallions, thinly sliced

DRESSING

½ cup mayonnaise

½ cup sour cream

2 tablespoons cider vinegar

1 teaspoon sugar

pinch of dry mustard

½ teaspoon salt

salt and pepper to taste

tools

sharp knife

cutting board

measuring cups & spoons

grater

large bowl

whisk

2 forks

Orange Vinaigrette Coleslaw

1 In a large bowl, whisk together all the Orange Vinaigrette Coleslaw **dressing** ingredients.

2 Add the cabbage, carrots, scallions, corn, and bell pepper. Toss with two forks to coat the vegetables with dressing. Let stand 30 minutes. Just before serving, add the cilantro and toss one more time.

Creamy Coleslaw

1 In a large bowl, whisk together all the Creamy Coleslaw dressing ingredients.

2 Add the cabbage, carrots, and scallions. Toss with two forks to coat the vegetables with dressing. Let stand 30 minutes. Toss again just before serving.

COOL TIP

You can make this up to one day ahead of time. Cover the bowl with plastic wrap and refrigerate until serving time. Be sure to toss once more before serving.

KICKIN' CHILE BROWNIES

ingredients

4 ounces unsweetened
 baking chocolate

1 cup butter

2 cups sugar

½ teaspoon salt

½ teaspoon baking powder

1 cup flour

2 tablespoons chile powder

2 tablespoons cinnamon

1 teaspoon vanilla

4 eggs, lightly beaten
 with a fork

tools

measuring cups

measuring spoons

fork

9 × 13-inch baking dish

small microwave-safe bowl

mixing spoon

large mixing bowl

rubber spatula

toothpick

1. Preheat the oven to 350 degrees. Coat the inside of the baking dish with butter. Sprinkle flour over the inside of the dish. Turn the dish upside down to remove any extra flour.

2. Put the chocolate and butter in a microwave-safe bowl. Cook for 1 minute on high. Take it out and stir it. If the chocolate isn't melted, cook for 30 seconds more. Stir again until the chocolate is completely melted.

3. Mix the sugar, salt, baking powder, flour, chile powder, and cinnamon in a large bowl.

4. Add the chocolate mixture, vanilla, and eggs. Mix well.

5. Spread the batter evenly in the baking dish.

6. Bake for 30 to 35 minutes. **Insert** a toothpick into the brownies. If it comes out clean, the brownies are done.

EVEN HOTTER HOT FUDGE

SERVES 8

ingredients

1 cup semi-sweet chocolate chips

salt

2 tablespoons butter, cut into bits

¼ cup heavy cream

1 teaspoon cinnamon

1 to 2 teaspoons chile powder

vanilla ice cream

tools

measuring cups

measuring spoons

small saucepan

rubber spatula

1. Put the chocolate chips, a **pinch** of salt, and ¼ cup water in a saucepan over medium-low heat. Stir constantly with a rubber spatula until the chocolate is melted. The chocolate and water should be completely blended to a smooth **consistency**.

2. Remove the pan from the heat and add the butter. Stir it in quickly.

3. Add half the cream and stir quickly until it is blended in. Add the rest of the cream and continue stirring quickly until the mixture is thick and shiny.

4. Stir in the cinnamon and 1 teaspoon of the chile powder. Taste the sauce. If you want it spicier, add another teaspoon of chile powder.

5. Let it cool slightly. Pour over ice cream and serve.

COOL TIP

Add ⅓ cup of crushed candy cane instead of chili powder to get a peppermint flavored hot fudge.

WATERMELON AGUA FRESCA

ingredients

1 cup sugar

6 cups cubed seedless watermelon

ice

1 lime, cut into wedges

tools

measuring cups

sharp knife

cutting board

small saucepan

mixing spoon

blender

2-quart pitcher

drinking glasses

1. Combine the sugar and 1 cup water in a small saucepan. Bring to a boil and stir until the sugar **dissolves**. Remove from heat and cool for 30 minutes.

2. Put half the watermelon and half the sugar mixture in a blender. Blend until smooth. Pour it into the **pitcher**. Repeat with the remaining watermelon and sugar mixture.

3. Stir well. Pour the drink into glasses filled with ice. **Garnish** with wedges of lime.

BEYOND COOL

- Make cantaloupe juice too! Just replace the cubed watermelon with the same amount of cubed cantaloupe.

GLOSSARY

consistency – how thick, firm, smooth, or sticky something is.

decrease – to make or become less, smaller, or fewer.

delicious – very pleasing to taste or smell.

dissolve – to mix with a liquid so that it becomes part of the liquid.

dressing – a sauce that is used in salads.

efficient – able to do something without wasting time, money, or energy.

garnish – to decorate a dish with small amounts of food.

glossary – a list of the hard or unusual words found in a book.

grate – to cut something into small pieces using a grater. A grater is a tool with sharp-edged holes.

insert – to stick something into something else.

mince – to cut or chop into very small pieces.

omit – to leave out.

permission – when a person in charge says it's okay to do something.

pinch – the amount of an ingredient that can be held between your finger and thumb.

pitcher – a container with a handle used to hold and pour liquids.

prep – short for preparation, the work done before starting to make a recipe, such as washing fruits and vegetables, measuring, cutting, peeling, and grating.

skillet – a frying pan.

supervision – the act of watching over or directing others.

taco – a fried or soft tortilla folded around a mixture of meat, cheese, tomato, and lettuce.

technique – a method or style in which something is done.

towel – a cloth or paper used for cleaning or drying.

utensil – a tool used to prepare or eat food.

varieties – different types of one thing.

version – a different form or type from the original.

WEB SITES

To learn more about cool cooking, visit ABDO Publishing Company online at www.abdopublishing.com. Web sites about cool cooking are featured on our Book Links page. These links are monitored and updated to provide the most current information available.

INDEX